Spain

A Traveler's Guide to the Must-See Cities in Spain!

By Sam Spector

Table of Contents

Introduction 5

Chapter 2: Bilbao 11

Chapter 3: Santiago de Compostela 15

Chapter 4: Madrid 19

Chapter 5: Toledo 23

Chapter 6: Córdoba 27

Chapter 7: Seville 32

Chapter 8: Granada 36

Chapter 9: Valencia 40

Chapter 10: Barcelona 44

Conclusion 49

Copyright 2015 by (Sam Spector) - All rights reserved.

This document is geared towards providing exact and reliable information in regards to the topic and issue covered. The publication is sold with the idea that the publisher is not required to render accounting, officially permitted, or otherwise, qualified services. If advice is necessary, legal or professional, a practiced individual in the profession should be ordered.

- From a Declaration of Principles which was accepted and approved equally by a Committee of the American Bar Association and a Committee of Publishers and Associations.

In no way is it legal to reproduce, duplicate, or transmit any part of this document in either electronic means or in printed format. Recording of this publication is strictly prohibited and any storage of this document is not allowed unless with written permission from the publisher. All rights reserved.

The information provided herein is stated to be truthful and consistent, in that any liability, in terms of inattention or otherwise, by any usage or abuse of any policies, processes, or directions contained within is the solitary and utter responsibility of the recipient reader. Under no circumstances will any legal responsibility or blame be held against the publisher for any reparation, damages, or monetary loss due to the information herein, either directly or indirectly.

Respective authors own all copyrights not held by the publisher.

The information herein is offered for informational purposes solely, and is universal as so. The presentation of the information is without contract or any type of guarantee assurance.

The trademarks that are used are without any consent, and the publication of the trademark is without permission or backing by the trademark owner. All trademarks and brands within this book are for clarifying purposes only and are the owned by the owners themselves, not affiliated with this document.

Introduction

Hi, my name is Sam and I first of all want to thank and congratulate you for purchasing my book, 'Spain: A Guide to the Must-See Cities in Spain!'

Spain is an undeniably beautiful country, with a passionate, proud people and an amazing landscape. Each of the cities in Spain offers something different to its visitors: from the unique, inspiring architecture of Barcelona, to the lively, eclectic culture of Valencia. All are unique in their own way, and have different sights and attractions to explore and enjoy.

The people you will meet along the way will approach you with a smile and a flash of fire in their eyes. The Spanish are proud, but exceptionally friendly and openly welcome tourists into their fantastic country.

There is so much to see in this extensive travel heaven, that you will wish you had more time to explore it all! Without the proper guidance, however, you won't get the chance to see everything that this phenomenal country has to offer you.

I will outline exactly how to get the most out of each of the best cities throughout Spain, and how to do this in a safe way. The adventures and exciting situations you will find yourself in throughout Spain are countless, and I will allow you to experience them all.

What I hope to achieve in this book is to provide you with a reliable guide on exactly what to see in each of Spain's major cities, and how to navigate your way around the country to see as much as humanly possible.

I will give you the top ten of my personal favorite things to see and do in each of the top ten cities in Spain, as well as a description of exactly why you simply can't miss them. I will provide insights that I've gained from my own extensive travel throughout Spain, and some tips for making the most out of your own Spanish adventure.

So allow me to show you all that Spain has to offer - its culture, sights and attractions - and you will have the trip of a lifetime!

Chapter 1: San Sebastián

Prepare to fall in love. As soon as you enter the charming, vibrant and utterly intoxicating city of San Sebastián, you will feel as if you have found a piece of yourself that has always been missing. The beaches, the food and the easy-going atmosphere of San Sebastián will sweep you off your feet and into its grasp, while the subtle intricacies of the city and its people will leave you hooked.

San Sebastián has some of the finest and most revered restaurants in the world, boasting a plethora of dining establishments adorned with Michelin Stars. The less lavish restaurants, cafes and shops all produce a fantastic array of food and local delicacies also, and you will never leave a meal feeling unsatisfied.

The bars throughout this vivid city are alive each and every night with a contagious excitement. The drinks are always flowing and the locals are always inviting and friendly, so you will have no qualms about letting your hair down and dancing your way through the many nights spent in San Sebastián.

By day the beaches of San Sebastián are both rare and magical. The golden sands of these beaches are the perfect place to relax and let your cares roam free as you watch the waves crashing on the shore, and the water itself produces perfect conditions for both some leisurely swimming and enjoyable surfing.

San Sebastián is truly a delight to visit and possesses a remarkable culture. The fun activities to participate in are endless, the people are friendly and the atmosphere is warm and inviting. Take your time to enjoy everything it has to offer, and don't feel too guilty when you realize that you don't actually ever want to leave.

The Top Ten

Playa de la Concha - To begin your exploration of the sizzling-hot San Sebastián, there is no better place than the beach! Playa de la Concha possesses everything a great city beach should have: golden sands, calm waters and a sea of tanned, golden bodies lining the shore. Many days can be spent at this popular beach soaking in the sunshine and frolicking in the water, and the beach provides the perfect setting to relax or have fun.

Isla de Santa Clara - Visible from Playa de la Concha itself, this little gem of an island provides an enjoyable trip across the bay. By boats sporting see-through glass bottoms you can travel to the island, gazing at the ocean floor beneath and any bright sea life you're lucky enough to spot. The island is fantastic for a stroll and has its own small beach to relax on in a more secluded environment.

Maria Cristina Bridge - While this bridge is not regarded as an attraction of the city, it certainly should be. This lovely ornamented structure is a delight to stroll across, and magnificent to gaze upon. The view from the bridge over the Urumea River is beautiful and the stonework of the structure is expertly created. Include this bridge on route to any other destination for an extra treat.

Monte Urgull - The views from atop this high mountain peak are nothing short of awe-inspiring. Taking a short walk from Playa de Zuloaga you will reach the summit to be greeted by a gigantic statue of Christ. This statue is a fantastic spectacle within itself, but the view is what really draws the crowds in. The castle sitting at the peak and its encompassing walls are also worth perusing while you are nearby.

Museo San Telmo - The city's most noteworthy museum holds a bit of everything. While it is technically a museum of Basque society and culture, the range of works include various historical artifacts, pieces of arts and displays of the different cultural periods throughout the Basque era.

Playa de Gros - Another of the fantastic beaches in San Sebastián, Playa de Gros is a beach with a bit more action. The waves can get slightly larger than elsewhere, and its cove provides the perfect setting for beginner and intermediate surfers to catch some waves. You can even get lessons right on the beach if you've never tried to surf before, and the local teachers will have you up on a wave in no time!

San Sebastián Cathedral - This epic cathedral is a hard sight to miss as you stroll by it. With a sharp main spire which protrudes high into the sky, seemingly cutting it in two, as you approach the structure it only becomes more and more daunting. Standing right beneath the main entrance and gazing up at the facade is fascinating, and the interior of the cathedral is delightful as well.

Monte Igueldo - The peak of Monte Igueldo provides a view which rivals any other to be found in Spain. An epic panorama awaits you upon reaching the summit, spanning the coast and mountains surrounding the mountain. The ride up to this mesmerizing view is exciting as well, as you can take the 'funicular railway' to the Parque de Atracciones which resides on the mountain top.

Restaurante Ni Neu - For dinner or lunch any hungry traveler in San Sebastián cannot avoid Restaurante Ni Neu. Situated directly beside and overlooking Playa de Gros, this establishment is a winner at any time of the day. The modern Spanish dishes on offer here are a real treat and will leave you wanting more - even though they are utterly satisfying.

Bar Ondarra - This very intimate and suave little bar is one of the jewels of San Sebastián and is one of the best places in the city to begin a night out. A glass of wine with good company here is one of the more relaxing and enjoyable times to be had in San Sebastián. Heading downstairs will expose you to a more eclectic taste in music, and one which will have you dancing into the early morning hours.

Chapter 2: Bilbao

Like a phoenix that has risen from the ashes, Bilbao is a shining light that has emerged from a dark and gloomy past.

The city of Bilbao began its journey as a dreary industrial city that was regarded as nothing more than a means for generating revenue and creating jobs for the people of Spain. Today it is a gleaming trophy of success against adversity, as it has transformed itself into one of the artistic centers of Spain.

There are more art museums in Bilbao per capita than just about anywhere in the World, each providing something different to the creative scene eminent in the city. This artistic flare is prevalent everywhere in Bilbao: from its street art installations, to its mesmerizing buildings and of course the wonderfully unique citizens.

More than just an epicenter for all things art, Bilbo boasts a character which is hard to replicate. Sea and mountain meet here to provide a clash of beautiful physical surroundings, and the seasonal produce and cuisine this combination brings to the city is an area which shows an artistic touch of the flavor variety.

Bilbao will leave you with a sense of your own creative abilities, and with a kiss of passion to light this flame within yourself once more.

The Top Ten

Museo Guggenheim - The glimmering crown in this city of artistic wonders is the esteemed Guggenheim Musuem. Many say that it is of a direct result of this structure that Bilbao was able to pull itself out of post-industrial depression and transform itself into the modern city it is today. The museum isn't particularly famous for its contents, however, although they are impressive. It is famous for its inspiring exterior, which is unparalleled in architectural wonder. A shifting assortment of curves and jagged edges, the Guggenheim is the shiny spacecraft which transported Bilbao into its bright future.

Museo de Bellas Artes - Not forgetting about all of the other wonderful museums Bilbao has to show off, the Museo de Bellas Artes is one of the finest. The three main categories of artwork constituting the permanent exhibits on offer are classical, contemporary and Basque, all of which are deeply interesting. The temporary exhibits displayed here are known to be of an extremely high quality also.

Casco Viejo - The old quarter of Bilbao is a charming assortment of colorful buildings, streets and sights. Tiny, independent shops little every corner and every crevice found within the quarters and there is an array of quintessential bars to be found in the area. Gazing up at the colorful apartment blocks with the inhabitants smiling down from their respective balconies is a surprisingly enjoyable experience.

Rio-Oja - Not for those possessing a light stomach or a closed mind, Rio-Oja is a restaurant which really implements a creative flare. With a menu including snails, squid, sheep brains and an assortment of other delightfully squeamish dishes, this restaurant is an interesting experience at the very least. The seafood on offer is a true delight, though, if you can't stomach any of the other specialties.

Funicular de Artxanda - You may not realize it walking about the quiet streets of Bilbao, but the city is situated amongst a breathtaking range of mountains that aren't quite visible from the valley floor. To view these spectacular surroundings, the funicular railway takes you to the very peak of Artxanda for a magical view of the city and the mountains encompassing it.

Museo Marítimo Ría de Bilbao - Yet another fantastic museum to be found in Bilbao is the Maritime Museum. Employing the power of light to illuminate the depths of the water in the surrounding waterfront, this museum displays the history of maritime in Bilbao in a spectacular show. Visitors can also traverse various boats and watercraft to view nautical structures at a closer range.

Mina Restaurante - At the epitome of fine dining in Bilbao sits Mina Restaurante; a fantastic excuse to indulge in some of most exquisite cuisine to be found in Basque culture. The dishes they offer are sumptuous and the restaurant itself is in a lavish setting. A booking is essential here but it is well worth the time to book a reservation.

Kafe Antzokia - This 'cafe' is a prime venue for some of the best musical acts to make their way to Bilbao. It regularly shows top-class rock and blues acts, and the concerts that are held in the venue are one of the most exciting experiences for the people of Bilbao. This quirky restaurant/cafe/concert hall will leave you impressed and entertained from any of the exciting shows you are able to visit here.

Rioja Wine Region - The Basque Country of Spain is renowned for its delectable wines and none more so than the Rioja Wine Region. A short drive from Bilbao, this region boasts an array of wineries that offer guided tours and samplings of their most delightful liquids. Be sure to either go on a tour or find a designated driver, so that you can truly indulge in all the region has to offer!

The Basque Coast - Another delightful area to explore on a day's outing from Bilbao is the Basque Coastline. This long stretch of coast possesses an interesting assortment of sights to stop and view, including the Transporter Bridge of Bizkaia and San Juan de Gaztelugatxe. The bridge is the oldest of its kind in the world, and a proud favorite of the locals. San Juan de Gaztelugatxe is a beautiful, large rock islet connected by a narrow bridge to the mainland, and its contrast with the stark coastline is a spectacular sight to behold.

Chapter 3: Santiago de Compostela

Stepping into this medieval, stone city is like stepping back in time itself. Walls, spires, rooftops and other glorious stone structures can be found lining the many streets of Santiago de Compstela.

The city has become popular in recent years due to it being a destination on the route of a popular pilgrimage across Spain. Hundreds of thousands of pilgrims and tourists venture toward Santiago de Compostela each year, to take in the beautiful scenery and breathtaking architecture found in this magnificent Spanish location.

There is a story also to be told in the history of this great city. Dating back to over a thousand years ago, Santiago de Compostela has seen apostles, kings and bishops pass through its streets. Today this history can be witnessed in the many fine structures erected in their honor, including churches and cathedrals that will leave you inspired by their beauty.

The Top Ten

Catedral de Santiago de Compostela - At the very crux of this amazing city sits the grand attraction that is the Catedral de Santiago de Compostela. The structure draws crowds worldwide to see its construction of stone architecture spanning several centuries and through different eras of cultural influence. It rises high above the city center and dominates much of the skyline, becoming even more impressive from up close. The highlights of the cathedral are the tomb of Santiago, which resides underneath the main altar within the church, and the many perfected stone sculptures which lie within the structure. There is a regular mass which takes place at midday for the religious pilgrims who have found their way to Santiago de Compostela.

Praza do Obradoiro - Nearby to the cathedral are many open, ostentatious plazas with many beautiful sights to view. The Praza do Obradoiro is the most delightful to behold, as you wander through its courtyards and admire the cathedral from yet another perspective, as well as the buildings surrounding it. The city hall sits alongside this main plaza, and is one of the many fine structures which line its perimeter.

Museo da Catedral - An attraction by its own right, yet in conjunction with the grand cathedral, is the cathedral museum. This museum spreads across four extensive floors to exhibit elaborate stone sculptures, tombs of deceased kings and many religious artifacts and artworks. Many people make the mistake of visiting the cathedral without viewing the museum, but the two should definitely go hand in hand.

Museo das Peregrinacións - Another museum in a short walking distance from the main cathedral is the Museo das Peregrinacións. This building provides a fantastic assortment of exhibits detailing the history of the Pilgrimage through Santiago, and the history of the city itself. While first and foremost a display of the city's history through artifacts and models, the building also provides yet another prime viewing location for the impressive nearby cathedral.

Alameda - A short distance from the historical center of Santiago de Compostela, this extremely gorgeous park area is a fine location to spend the day. When the weather is nice, you can roam about its grounds for hours on end, amongst the lines of perfectly structured trees. As from almost everywhere in the city, you can also see the large towers of the cathedral poking up above the green treetops, which is an excellent view as you relax upon the grass.

Colexio de Fonseca - Hidden to the south of the cathedral, within the Praza de Fonseca, sits an exquisite part of the original Santiago University. Now open to view for any tourists who wander through the area, the courtyard within this section is breathtaking to behold, and expertly structured. The surrounding area of the plaza is also enjoyable to explore, with a multitude of eclectic cafes to visit.

Mercado de Abastos - With hundreds of lively, exciting stalls setup selling a plethora of meats, produce, pastries and seafood to indulge in, this city market is a must-see stop on any tour of Santiago de Compostela. People flood to this market at all times of the day to buy the freshest foods and ingredients to be found within the city, and the scene here is always electric and extremely diverse.

Mariscomanía 10% - With your freshly-bought produce from the market, there is only one thing to do: cook and eat! Being on holidays it is natural not to want to do this cooking yourself, and luckily there is an alternative to have it expertly prepared for you. At Mariscomanía 10% the chefs will take your ingredients of meat or seafood and elect to cook it for you in an expert fashion, allowing you to return half and hour later to enjoy it. With beers and wine also on offer this is the perfect way to enjoy a meal in the city.

Garigolo - Super hip, cool and relaxed cafe by day; a rocking, electric concert venue by night. Garigolo is an interesting contradiction of vibes, as it provides an enjoyably calm demeanor throughout the day to enjoy good company and food, whereas at night you can go wild to the rhythm of local artists and bands. Whenever you arrive you are sure to have a good time, but it's best to experience the best of both worlds.

Modus Vivendi - A venue purely oriented around hardcore partying is Modus Vivendi. Set in the stables of a former mansion, this club hosts both live music and DJs regularly, and is a popular place to party at an extreme level. There is generally a younger crowd found within this club/pub type venue, but it is thoroughly enjoyable for all ages.

Chapter 4: Madrid

No city has more energy, more passion and more sheer personality than this Spanish gem. Everything that embodies Spain is found within this beloved Spanish city; a lively and passionate people, a unique and proud culture and a fierce atmosphere of utter enjoyment everywhere you look.

This city is made for fun. By day you can walk through the streets, without ever being dulled by the glorious array of mesmerizing architecture and interesting local types. The art collections to be found here rival any other major city throughout Europe and indeed the world, and the cuisine in Madrid is nothing short of a culinary miracle.

By night the city transforms itself into a whirlwind adventure of music, dance and an intent to have fun at all times. Forever optimistic you will remain about the night scene in Madrid, and you will be surprised by the volume of bars and clubs you will be carried along to before the night finally comes to an end. From sunrise to sunset, this is truly a magical city to behold.

The Top Ten

Círculo de Bellas Artes - This center for culture is one of the finest places in Madrid to get a feel for the lifestyle of the city. It is a multifaceted, interdisciplinary organization which displays exhibitions, films and concerts, among other forms of artistic expression. Overall it provides a look into every aspect of cultural lifestyle of Madrid, and is constantly shifting as with the exhibits on display.

Parque del Buen Retiro - For a look into the most spectacular gardens to be found in any European city, El Retiro is the place to go. With a beautiful artificial lake at its center, you can venture outward to explore its green grounds, abundance of fountains, stone sculptures and many paths. The park is a favorite place for both locals and tourists to visit at every time of the year and the vibe here is always friendly and welcoming. Whether viewing the roses in its stunning garden, taking a boat ride or simply relaxing in the shade, this park is a marvel that must be experienced.

Plaza de Santa Ana - This main plaza could be deemed the culmination of Madrid culture in one single location. The atmosphere in Plaza de Santa Ana is friendly and contagious, with many locals mingling and enjoying the pleasant surroundings. There are many interesting cafes in the area, and the buildings in the plaza are enough to inspire a creative urge unlike any other. At any time of the day this plaza is lined with people, and there is always something exciting in the air here.

Mercado de San Miguel - Entwined within the history of the city, this popular locals market is both ancient and beautiful. Among the hum drum of the daily routine of buying and selling, there is also a variety of delectable Spanish tapas to indulge in. From as little as 1 Euro, you can sit amongst the tables strewn throughout the markets and dine upon a feast of small dishes, while watching the day-to-day haggling of produce and knick-knacks take place. You can choose to sample wines, fresh fruits, cheese and even omelettes: the possibilities are endless! It is a truly unforgettable experience.

Café Central - Continuously regarded as one of the world's best jazz bars, this cruisy club is a must-see on any music lover's list.

It has hosted thousands of top notch gigs throughout its history as Madrid's finest smoky jazz club, and has every type of jazz imaginable on offer. The food in the club is also fantastic, so leave room for a meal, but don't eat so much that you can't get up and have a dance along to the smooth tunes!

Sobrino de Botín - To dine in a world-class, world-renowned and world record holding restaurant, there is no substitute for Sobrino de Botín. This immaculate restaurant is recognized as the oldest restaurant in the entire world - established in 1725. Over the span of three centuries, this fine dining establishment has learned a thing or two about culinary creativity, and knows how to make one's palette dance with delight. Although slightly on the pricey side and although overrun with tourists, this restaurant is more than worth a visit for its charm and its truly delicious meals.

Estado Puro - In a city as dripping with culinary delights as Madrid, it is not surprising to find yourself constantly full yet forever hungry, and Estado Puro is part of the cause of this dilemma. Another of the many fantastic tapas bars to be found in the city, Estado Puro offers a few different varieties of tapas than you would find normally, including cod balls and Jamon Croquettes, but provides a delightful taste experience nonetheless. The design of the bar is appealing and the vibe is often calm, sophisticated and always laid back. Although it sits a little outside the main city center, this tapas bar is worth it for the fine food and engaging atmosphere.

Museo Chicote - Some would call this a roaring bar, others would say that it is a true Madrid landmark. I would say that it is both. At any time of the night you could potentially find any character or personality enjoying one of the hundreds of cocktails on offer, from locals and tourists to one of the many celebrities which frequent the bar. The interior has a swanky '20s vibe to it, and gets quite cosy in the late hours despite the DJs pumping out tune after tune.

DiverXO - Dining for the elite isn't something I normally partake in nor that I would recommend to any traveler, but sometimes one must simply treat oneself. The best place to do such is at DiverXO. With main meals set at over $100, this is certainly a very fine dining experience, but one you won't regret. The restaurant is Madrid's only 3-Michelín Star dining venue, attributed due to its tantalizing albeit unusual meals. The entire dining experience is interactive and fun, as the chefs put the finishing touches to the food as you are enjoying it! Bookings up to 6 months in advance are necessary, so planning ahead is essential if you want to enjoy this once in a lifetime opportunity.

Sala El Sol - To close any Madrid night off, after a meal and a leisurely walk about town to soak in the rare after-dark treasures, you should be in an ideal mood to shake it at Sala El Sol. This venue hosts regular concerts of an extremely broad variety, after which the house DJ takes to the decks to guide you into the ecstasy of the early morning.

Chapter 5: Toledo

Despite its small size and relatively inexistent tourist following, Toledo is an undiscovered cultural wonder for anyone who stumbles upon it. Set high atop a hill with the beautiful Castilla-La Mancha plains surrounding it, the city is like something out of a fairytale.

The city's existence as a multi-cultural, historic, religious melting pot gives it a rather unique quality that few other cities can mimic. With its possession of a multitude of medieval religious structures, including Jewish, Christian and Arabic just to name a few, the city acts as one large museum to educate on the history of many world religions.

Toledo has quite a sullen past as well. It was one of the main cities involved in the persecutions of various anti-Catholics during the Spanish Inquisition, and is remembered as a symbol of medieval religious society.

Today Toledo represents a spectacle of religious and architectural wonder, as you pass by the many buildings and through the labyrinth-structured streets in between, you will be amazed at the diverse nature of the city. This forgotten treasure is one that you surely won't want to miss.

The Top Ten

Toledo Cathedral - The main Catholic cathedral of Toledo should definitely be the first stop on your religious pilgrimage through the city. Walking toward the structure you will find yourself in awe of the beautiful facade and towers connected to the main structure. Walking inside your jaw will continue to drop lower and lower, as you walk past treasure after treasure in the various rooms. Gold is a common theme in the cathedral, with everything from gold leaves to gold paintings. The golden altar is certainly the winner, however, amongst a lavishly spacious room and thick stone columns; it is an amazing spectacle.

Mezquita del Cristo de la Luz - The Mosque of Christ of the Light has a subtlety to it, which although not as ostentatious as the cathedral, certainly possesses a captivating amount of beauty. As the last remaining Mosque of the city (at over 1000 years old), it holds a special place in the heart of many locals. It's interesting to contrast both the architectural and spiritual differences between this and the other religious structures throughout Toledo.

Sinagoga del Tránsito - Yet another impressive religious structure, this Jewisg Synagogue has been restored to its former 14th century glory, and is one of the most structurally impressive buildings in Toledo. It also contains a museum within its walls, Museo Sefardí, providing a rare look into Jewish culture in Spain, and highlighting their persecution by Catholics throughout the 15th century. The gardens provide a relaxing change to walk through as well, and the entire walking tour is a rather intimate experience.

Monasterio de San Juan de los Reyes - This famous monastery is an absolute delight to walk about, and is engrained in the religious history of the city. Initially built in the heart of the Jewish quarter as an insult by Catholic monarchs, it is clearly visible and contains several overt Catholic sculptures and symbols. The many arches, sculptures and pillars are amazingly designed, and the rose garden is a beautiful addition.

Plaza de Zocodover - The best spot in town for people watching is at Plaza Zocodover. Here you can rest in the shade of the many trees and watch both the world and the cheery locals go by, for hours on end. There is an array of fine dining spots surrounding the plaza, and several nice places to stop in for a coffee. If you've been meaning to get a bit of shopping done while in Toledo, this would also be the place to do it!

Alcázar - Looming high above the city of Toledo sits the domineering Alcázar, a military museum which spans several centuries' worth of history. This museum is enormous in terms of size, and comprehensive in terms of its contents. Everything to do with the Spanish military can be found here, including uniforms, relics, weaponry and exhibits explaining various significant military movements which have shaped Spain.

Pedro Maldonado Gonzalez - The city of Toledo has long been revered for its production of weaponry for the Spanish army and its rulers, particularly in the creation of swords. Everywhere you walk on the street you will find stalls set up selling their wares to tourists, all in varying qualities and prices. Pedro Maldonado Gonzalez is a fine souvenir shop which includes one of the largest arrays of these beauties found in Toledo. Their swords and other trinkets shimmer as if brand new, and you can purchase one of your very own for a reasonable price - just be wary of taking it on the plane ride home!

Termas Romanas - The ruins and remains of Toldeo's Roman Baths provide an interesting look back in time at former Toledo. Although the Baths are run-down and there is not much left of them, they are still well worth viewing just to picture what ancient Toledo was like so many years ago. There is also a very interesting collection of artworks featured here, including several sketches from big names such as Picasso and Miró, as well as several sketches of Toledo itself.

Museo de Santa Cruz - It is rewarding when you find that the way an art museum is designed is a work of art within itself, and this is the case at Museo de Santa Cruz. Here you can walk its beautiful corridors and hallways and gaze up at Spanish works of art which span across the many eras the country has seen. Many Spanish monarchs are featured in the exhibits, and the section of El Greco paintings is especially impressive.

Kumera - A restaurant which takes a new approach to traditional local cuisine: this is what you will find at Kumera. It has arguably the best food for its price range within this region of Spain, serving up the likes of suckling pig for a fraction of the price you will find it elsewhere. Their set menu is particularly enticing, and allows you to experience a wide variety of their many fine dishes for a low price. The atmosphere is relaxed and the staff are friendly, which makes the whole experience so enjoyable you may find yourself coming back several times before your trip is through!

Chapter 6: Córdoba

This rich, vibrantly cultural city has a powerful history with more milestone achievements than any other in Spain and indeed much of Europe. Córdoba was once the most elite city in the Western world, and holds the title for the very first university established in Europe. Today there is a largely commercial situation present in Cordoba, but it still maintains its luster of times past, with its ancient cobble stone streets, fountains, stoned gateways and glorious buildings.

Exploring this city by foot is the only real way to soak in all that it has to offer. Strolling through the more aging sections provides an experience unlike any other, allowing you to be transported back to a time when Córdoba was shaping the future of the modern world. These sections are also in stark juxtaposition to each other, as you step from the more Islamic quarters into the Jewish quarter, the layout and structures change instantly, as does the atmosphere.

The many glorious plazas to explore will fill your day with wonder, as you hop from cafe to restaurant to bar within each one. The locals you will find on your travels are welcoming and inviting, and they too seem as if they have seen the coming and going of many influential movements within this once powerful city. Exploring this medieval city of wonder is an experience not to be missed, so I encourage you to explore it all while you have the chance!

The Top Ten

Mezquita - The most lavish and alluring sight in Córdoba is undoubtedly the famous Córdoba Mosque. This structure is a picture of elegance and beauty, representing a time when the Arab influence in Spain was very strong, particularly in this part of the country. It powerfully outlines how religions can exist side by side in peace, with the Christian cathedral and place of worship residing right alongside its Islamic counterpart. The structure can be seen from far away, although is even more magnificent up close. The Mosque is at its most impressive at night, when the lights shining upon it glow in an orange hue which makes the building take on a magical air.

Concurso de Patios Cordobeses – Cordoba citizens love their patios, and they are on show in all their glory during the month of May each year. At this time the many patios of the houses which line every street are lush with colorful flowers and plants, and many are entered in this annual competition. They are open to public viewing during this time, and walking around the city exploring them all is a real treat. At all other times of the year there are a few of the larger patios which remain open for viewing, although the flowers may not be blooming it is remarkable to see the effort locals go to in maintaining their precious patios.

Judería - The characteristic Jewish Quarter of Córdoba has a number of eclectic sights and scenes to partake in. You could spend an entire day exploring this part of the city, drinking in the unique culture of the district. The white buildings with colorful flowers hanging from every window is a sight to behold, while the smiles of the people peering out of these windows is the real treasure. The Judaic-Spanish traditional is still alive and well in Judería, and everyone who visits Córdoba should experience it.

Casa Mazal - Sticking to the Jewish theme, this fine Jewish restaurant is an experience that you will be hard-pressed to find elsewhere throughout Spain. It mixes elements of several different cultural influences, including the likes of Italian and African cooking, to create a wide variety of delectable kosher foods to enjoy. Many of the best dishes are vegetarian, and are overwhelmingly flavorsome.

Museo Arqueológico - This quaint little museum is a hidden gem on the map of Córdoba. It gives a very intricate account of the history of Córdoba, from the very initiation of the city up until the present day. During the construction of the museum, the remains of a Roman Theater were found by chance, and these are explained in an exhibit of their very own which you can walk through in the building's basement.

Madinat al-Zahra - If you are a lover of history or architecture, and especially if you love both, then you cannot miss the opportunity to experience Madinat al-Zahra. These historical ruins, along with the museum contained within, allow you to view an enormous display of excavated Roman Palace and dwellings kept in reasonable condition considering the numerous plundering for materials over the years. This astounding archaeological site allows visitors to view the Palace and imagine it as it was at the height of its glory, over 1000 years ago.

Patio de los Naranjos - This leafy, green courtyard which resides just outside of the Mezquita is a sight to behold. Named for its abundance of vibrant orange trees, this courtyard has had a significant influence on the city and the western world in general. The minaret which was built here set the path for the design of all Islamic minarets there after because of its sheer beauty and architectural perfection. Walking through this courtyard is a serene experience, and if you manage to visit alone can seem like a respite from the real world.

Palacio de Viana - This breathtaking Renaissance-styled palace is intimidatingly beautiful and ostentatious, being the most perfectly maintained structure of its kind within the city. The private mansion now is open to anyone for viewing, and includes and interesting museum with remarkable artwork contained therein. The real treasure is the building itself, and its possession of amazing patios and spectacular courtyards. The patios of Palacio de Viana are regarded as the most beautiful of their kind in the world, and something you truly have to experience to appreciate fully.

Cervezas Califa - While microbreweries aren't something the Spanish are generally renowned for, this established brewery is staking its claim at creating the best beer in Spain. The extensive beer menu and the friendly bar atmosphere makes this microbrewery a truly unforgettable experience, and one which really has you hoping that it can take on the big names in beer brewing. It's a perfect place to stop after a long walk around the city; to relax and unwind after a long day.

Bodega Guzman - If beer isn't your drink of choice, but you still would like to enjoy some of the entertaining venues of the city of Córdoba, Bodega Guzman has got you covered. Huge barrels of fine Spanish wine hide behind the bar, constantly being emptied into the many glasses of tourists and locals that fill the venue. The space is covered in bull fighting memorabilia, and really feels like a true, somewhat rough, Spanish bar with a hearty warmth to it.

Chapter 7: Seville

The flame of passion burns bright in this southern Spanish metropolis, known as one of the original proponents of the saucy flamenco dance. In every bar and every restaurant the music for this fiery dance will be playing, and the locals need no encouragement to show their skilled dancing and excitable nature.

The adventurous atmosphere is contagious within Seville, and everywhere you go you will find a flare of artistic brilliance to inspire you, a romantic pair gazing deep into each other's eyes or a heated discussion between locals over a glass of wine. This passion is contagious, and you will find yourself moved by this city and its people.

The beauty of this Andalucian city dates back to (according to myth) around 3000 years ago, and has been getting more and more beautiful ever since. The castle complex in Seville is the height of its wonder, being a marvel of Gothic architecture, but the combined magnificent of each and every building in Seville provides a viewing experience like no other.

Seville is a sexy combination of character and beauty, and is one that will leave its mark on all who visit it. Come here to mingle with locals, dance the flamenco and feel utterly alive for every second in this great Spanish city.

The Top Ten

Alcázar - Possibly the most spectacular, illuminating and unforgettable sight you will be privileged enough to behold on your Spanish journey rests within the walls of Alcázar. The architecture present in this former fort is nothing short of remarkable, as it has constantly been updated and improved upon over the centuries by various rulers. Its greatest features were added in the 14th century during the dark ages, and still remain present today. The many patios, chambers and gardens of this illustrious palace are a sight which will leave you wishing you could be an ancient Spanish monarch, just for one day, so all of it could be yours.

Seville Cathedral - This immense, domineering and utterly impressive cathedral holds the official title of largest cathedral in the entire world. Its sheer size is inconceivable until you actually walk through its vast halls and chambers and experience the height and magnitude of the structure. Taking a tour of the cathedral you will be able to visit the final resting place of Christopher Columbus, and be completely enthralled by the grandeur of the building, especially its Gothic facade and its colorful stained glass windows.

Giralda - Sitting to the north-east of the cathedral is the vast Giralda Tower. This ancient bell tower is over 100m in height and has overlooked the cathedral for over 800 years. There is a set of ramps which lead up to the top, so the ascent is quite manageable. When you reach the top you will be shocked at how high you've actually climbed, as you peer out with a remarkable panoramic view out over Seville.

Parque de María Luisa - This huge park is packed full of wonderful nature and highlights the wonderful culture present in Seville. Strolling through the María Luisa Park on a hot day is wonderful to gaze at the plants and people enjoying the weather, and there is an abundance of shade about if the sun becomes too much. There are countless paths to explore throughout the park, and even some serene ponds to feed the ducks.

Plaza de España - Sitting just to the south of María Luisa Park is this gorgeous, vast plaza. It faces directly opposite the park, and is surrounded by a cluster of inspiring historical buildings. Here there is also a concentration of beautiful doves at all times of the day to feed and admire, along with a dense concentration of locals enjoying the atmosphere. The tile work around the Plaza is the most lavish in the city, and has a flare unlike any other Plaza you can find in Spain.

Torre del Oro - This grand 'Tower of Gold' is said to have once possessed a dome that was covered in gold so bright that it shined brightly from miles away. Today it is lacking the gold, but is still an impressive work of architecture. It was once used to store treasures gained by the Spanish Conquistadors, and today houses a small maritime museum. Although the museum is nothing spectacular, the tower itself is definitely worth visiting.
Aire de Sevilla - After a long day walking around exploring and enjoying the many sights and scenes of Seville, you may need to relax a little to recuperate. There is no better place to do this than Aire de Sevilla, a set Moorish baths facility which provides utter tranquility and relaxation to visitors. The ambiance of this bathhouse is unmatched throughout Seville, and the on-site tea house adds even more to the experience.

Museo del Baile Flamenco - The history and significance of flamenco dance is explained and illustrated in grand fashion within the Museo del Baile Flamenco. The museum displays the dance as more of an art form, and includes verious sketches, costumes and other materials used in the art of flamenco dance. The highlight has to be the performances by professionals of the flamenco dance, who tell stories using this craft in a spectacular fashion, which makes you desperately want to learn to dance as well as them - luckily they also do classes (for a price).

Metropol Parasol - This work of architectural wonder and boldness, claimed by many as the 'flying waffle', sits above one of Seville's main shopping districts and is a pure delight to witness. It is claimed to be the largest wooden building in the world, and is impressive without even taking into account its vast size. The curves and waves of the structure are unique and creative, but somehow manage to blend in with the city around it. The beautiful views of the city skyline from the structure are just another reason to visit.

Vinería San Telmo - This is what I would call tapas with a twist. The variety and creativity of the dishes present in this famous Seville tapas restaurant make it one of the most unique restaurants in the city, and the most enjoyable by a large margin. There signature dish is the rascocielo, which is a skyscraper constructed of salmon, goat's cheese, eggplant and tomatoes, and is nothing short of pure food heaven.

Chapter 8: Granada

For a deep, engaging look into Spain's Moorish culture there is no substitute for the historical and architectural wonder of Granada. The Alhambra fortress is at the heart of the exploration of Granada, and the Moorish old quarter provides the most interesting insights into former Moorish life in Spain.

As you continue your exploration further out from this ancient center, however, you will begin to notice shifts in the way the city is designed, and the development of the city toward the modern age is directly tangible as you look around.

Sitting atop a peak and surrounded by the pristine Sierra Nevada mountains, the location of this great city is unparalleled in beauty. With the coastline of Spain a short trip by car away, you can even pop to the beach for the day before returning to enjoy the Granada nightlife.

Oh and you will enjoy the nightlife! For such a small city the night activities and festivities can pack a real punch. Hopping from bar to bar, enjoying tapas, wines and dancing in quick succession, you'll understand exactly why the locals seem so content and tourists are never disappointed with a visit to this amazing city.

The Top Ten

Alhambra - This historic palace is highly regarded in Granada as the most beautiful sight the city has to offer, and a true tribute to the picturesque Sierra Nevada Mountains surrounding the city.

As one of the most visited sights in Spain, with thousands of daily visitors passing to and from its walls, upon entry it is not hard to see why. It is a work of architectural genius, a colorful assortment of stone and tile melded into one phenomenal structure. The views from atop the Alhambra are also unequaled, making the whole experience truly amazing.

Granada Cathedral - Another of the beauitful structures found in Granada is the city's main cathedral. The building has been constructed in various styles, with the interior possessing a Renaissance theme while the exterior is mostly of Baroque influence. The result is a truly unique building, both inside and out, and this is certainly not 'just another cathedral'.

Capilla Real - Joined to the Granada Cathedral at the hip is the magnificent Capilla Real. Built as a royal mausoleum for the Catholic monarchs Isabella I and Ferdinand II, the structure is now a popular tourist attraction alongside the cathedral, because of its beauty and possession of historical artifacts. The mini museum within the building houses Isabella's scepter, Ferdinand's sword and an assortment of other family arts and treasures.

Monastery of Saint Jerome - This Roman Catholic church holds a kind of peaceful beauty and tranquility which is hard to find elsewhere. As you walk through the elaborately decorated structure, throughout its carefully throughout and spacious rooms, you will find yourself quietly reflecting how lucky you are to be present in the structure. The central patio is a particular delight, filled with lush orange trees and beautifully kept.

Albayzín - The old Muslim quarter of Granada provides both an interesting cultural experience, and a fantastic adventure of exploration. The winding cobblestone streets of this neighborhood go up and down and all over the place, between stunning buildings and down mysterious alleys. The view from some points in the area is spectacular across Granada as well, and there is sure to be a few locals walking about who may be able to tell you their own personal story about the quarter.

El Ají - Within this pleasant Muslim quarter resides and equally pleasant and enjoyable dining experience. El Ají is a tiny quintessential Spanish restaurant with overtly friendly staff who do their best to make each of their customer's dining experience as pleasant as possible. You can choose to eat their all-day breakfast or indulge in Tequila-covered prawns. Whatever you choose you can rest easy knowing that the chef makes every dish as perfect as possible and customer satisfaction is the number one priority.

Mirador de San Nicolás - The hike to the top of this wondrous attraction is well worth it, for even just a glimpse at one of the most breathtaking sights to experience in Granada. As you gaze out from Mirador de San Nicolás you will witness the best view of Alhambra from afar as well as over Granada in its entirety. If you can manage to stay until around sunset, you will be in for a real treat as the sun dips down below Alhambra for a truly magical experience.

Le Chien Andalou - With a particularly 'pub' type atmosphere, this esteemed venue regularly pumps out smash acts of flamenco dance and music to the delight of its adoring crowd. Constantly crowded with locals and tourists, it is a hot spot to view live music and party into the night. If you've never had the opportunity to experience the traditional Spanish flamenco, you would be doing yourself a disservice not to view it here first. The acts are both authentic and thoroughly enjoyable.

Boogaclub - After you've had your fill of the saucy flamenco, and in a mood for a bit of a boogie yourself, look no further than Boogaclub. This club has a variety of music including funk, soul, jazz and reggae. DJs take to the floor each night to help you party until the early hours, and the floor is constantly packed with locals and tourists out for a wild time.

Sierra Nevada - While in one of the most naturally pristine pieces of land in the world, it would be a crime not to explore them properly. With Granada as a focal point, you can head in just about any direction and see some remarkable scenery. By car there are many roads and routes where you can travel, with no destination in mind, and simply allow yourself to take in the wilderness in front of you. Just remember to keep in mind the way to get back to Granada, and then allow yourself to experience the beauty of the mountains around you.

Chapter 9: Valencia

A mixed bag of art, culture and excitement awaits you upon your arrival to Valencia. The city is a wonderful concoction of so many fantastic Spanish cultures with a modern edge to them, reflected in the subtle, futuristic look of the buildings within it.

The City of Arts and Sciences within Valencia is a central point for exploration; one which is the highlight of the city and one of the prime reasons so many tourists come to visit each year. Much more than arts and science alone, however, Valencia also possesses an array of fantastic beaches and a laid back Mediterranean vibe.

One of the most remarkable aspects of the city is its creativity in the way it has been structured and designed. The former riverbed of the Turia, which was constantly flooding and subsequently diverted, was converted into a beautiful park which winds its way throughout the city. Such innovation is typical of the forward-thinking and creative Valencia.

This city contains everything you could ever need: food, great people, a fun nightlife and an amazing culture. It is undoubtedly one of the most genuine cities in Spain, and a favorite Spanish city of many who are blessed enough to visit.

The Top Ten

Museo de las Ciencias Príncipe Felipe - Contained within the epic City of Arts and Sciences, the Principe Felipe Science Museum is one of the major attractions and akey constituent of this futuristic structures. The building itself is amazing, being a work of genius, and the science exhibits found within it are engaging and informative. Although perhaps suited more to a slightly younger crowd, the museum is certainly worth seeing.

Oceanogrŕfic - Another major attraction within the City of Arts and Sciences, this mega aquarium is the highlight of many visitors to Valencia: both young and old. As you walk through its underwater tunnels (ranging up to 70m in length), you'll feel as if you've somehow become submerged under the ocean, with an array of fish and other sea creatures gazing at you and swimming straight past.

Jardins del Turia - Spanning the length of the former River Turia, the riverbed has been converted into a park filled with bike paths, beautiful greenery, fields and playgrounds. It is one of the Valencia's proudest attractions, and one that is dominated by locals on sunny days. You can choose to explore its entire 9km length, or view just a small portion, but know that whatever activity you choose within this wonderful park you will allow you to have an amazing time.

Bioparc - A zoo is typically not on any list of must-see tourist attractions for travelers, but the Valencia Bioparc is a zoo with a twist. The park is completely ecofriendly and has enclosures which are much larger than a typical zoo, allowing the animals to roam about more freely. The enclosures are also highly replicated to the animals' natural habitats, and the Bioparc does the best job possible at ensuring the animals are as comfortable and safe as possible.

Valencia Cathedral - Another Spanish city and yet another inspiring cathedral. The structure of Valencia's cathedral is unlike those in the previous cities, with a more subtle facade of plain stone. Subtle certainly doesn't mean boring, however, as the facade contains several expertly carved sculptures amidst a remarkable stone archway at the entrance. Upon entry to the cathedral the alter immediately catches the eye with the presence of several beautiful paintings and golden chandeliers.

Museo de Bellas Artes - This museum is featured amongst the top museums in Spain, and is a true highlight of the city of Valencia. There is an abundance of world-famous art pieces, with the specialties of the museum being in the several huge mosaics that feature throughout its rooms. The architecture in this facility is worth noting also, with an immense, bright blue dome encapsulating the building.

Torres de Quart - This set of ancient gates has been left in place as a historic reminder of the former Valencia. It is the most notable city gate in Spain, and has lasted through many years and through the French invasion of Valencia led by Napoleon. You can climb the steps to the top and gaze outward over the city, toward the setting sun if the time is right. Climbing to the top of the structure provides an even better view, and its often not crowded either.

Mercado Central - The main market of Valencia still maintains the feel of an ancient market where haggling, yelling and bargaining are all part of the routine, but the scene is one of a modern flare; a structure of intricate design and class. As you walk through the many stalls the smells and sounds mingle together to create a wonderful sensual sensation. In the middle of the market sits a tapas bar where you can drink in the atmosphere and taste some of the best food the market has on offer.

Delicat - For a more intimate experience of Spanish tapas within Valencia, the Delicat tapas restaurant is an excellent option. In stark contrast to the many flashy, overcrowded and tourist-luring tapas bars, this restaurant is hidden down a small street and has only enough room for a handful of people. What they lack in size, they certainly make up for in flavor. Showcasing the many wonderful local foods of Valencia, the dishes are innovative and unique; just like Valencia.

Pacha Valencia - When night falls, dinner has been had and you are suddenly in the mood for a party, Pacha Valencia beckons. This enormous venue can pack in over 1000 patrons to its main floor, who can dance wildly to the music pumped out by the local and international DJs who feature throughout the night. Being able to hold so many people enables the club to deal with the large demand on most nights of the week, but it's best to turn up reasonably early just to be safe.

Chapter 10: Barcelona

The crowning jewel on any trip around Spain is undoubtedly Barcelona. A city of magic unrivaled by any of its Spanish metropolis counterparts, this large city manages to maintain a feel of indifference to its own size, with the atmosphere and enthusiasm of a small, young Spanish town, yet all of the amazing sights of a well-seasoned capital.

The city is an intoxicating mix of colors and stunning architecture, with its on unique style to it unlike any of the larger cities in Spain. Colored tiles make a regular appearance in the design of buildings in the main part of the city, which excite the eye and add a special flare to the ancient structures of the city. The architectural wonders present in Barcelona date back as far as two millennia, and many of the buildings are entrenched in the history of the country.

Despite its prominent place in Spanish history, the city maintains a cool, calm seaside vibe, thanks to its close proximity to the Mediterranean. The beach side bliss of Barcelona's many popular districts is reason enough for the locals to spend much of their time swimming and frolicking in the deep blue Mediterranean waters and bathing on the sun-drenched sands. Tourists love to relax at the beaches too, and enjoy the many restaurants, bars and clubs in close proximity to these areas.

The food is fantastic, the people are crazy (in a good way) and the parties are endless in Barcelona. The Bohemian bars, intimate tapas restaurants, astounding architecture and world class clubs are but a few of the countless reasons to visit this amazing city, and you will discover plenty more that will tempt you to stay forever.

The Top Ten

La Sagrada Família - The sight of this medieval cathedral will either inspire you beyond words, or haunt your dreams! As you stand beneath La Sagrada Família, with the spires of this gigantic structure towering up into the sky, you feel minuscule by comparison. The tall spires can be seen from miles away, and as you approach and the facade comes into focus, your draw begins to drop more and more at the sight of this breathtaking church. The interior is just as beautiful, with stained glass windows, cavernous halls and rich, tasteful decor. This is Spain's most visited monument for a reason, and the reason is that it is undeniably beautiful.

La Rambla - Paris is famous for the Champs-Élysées, and Barcelona for its own popular and world-renowned main strip. La Rambla runs directly through the heart of Barcelona, and has everything you could ever want in a main street. Buskers, performers, artists, mimes and a vivid combination of locals and tourists scrambling about at all times of the day. Due to its steady gradient, the street is a popular location for skaters to cruise down as well, which is fun to watch from a cafe table. The entire middle section of the street is a pedestrian strip, where you can sit, relax and take in the true Catalan culture around you.

Casa Batlló - Amongst the recurring colorful and innovative architecture that Barcelona is famous for, there are a few buildings which put the rest to shame out of sheer creativity. Casa Batlló is one such building; a fairytale structure which is a mismatch of shapes, covered in a splash of colored paints with the result being something which is wacky, exciting and architecturally astounding.

Museu Picasso - This art museum is unlike any other you will have visited before: and not just because of the comprehensive amount of genius artworks within it. The museum is set in a series of medieval stone mansions which are a delight to walk through as you gain a deep insight into the mind and life of one of the world's greatest ever artists. The huge number of works within the museum focus mainly on Picasso's early works, and although it doesn't feature those which are regarded as his greatest masterpieces, the number of severely impressive works is enough to impress anyone.

Camp Nou - The people of Catalan are a passionate group, no more so than when it comes to sport. Barcelona FC is one of the most passionately followed football teams in the world, and have earned their fans undying appreciation many times over. Camp Nou is the home of this mighty sporting outfit, and a remarkable sight to visit to experience some sporting culture. If you get the chance to view the team play at their home ground, you're in for an unforgettable experience as the home crowd roars like a jet engine for 90 straight minutes. Even if you can't make a game, a tour of the ground is amazing to learn the team's history and glorious past victories.

Basílica de Santa Maria del Mar - As the second-most beautiful cathedral in Barcelona, you can't help but feel that the Basilica has been cheated by being placed in the same city as La Sagrada Familia. In any other city it would surely be the standout. This beautiful Gothic church isn't as lavish as La Sagrada Familia, but it makes up for it in its clear-cut, and structurally beautiful facade. The interior is similar, aside from its bright, stained glass windows, and is rarely crowded.

Park Guell - A living work of art is what you'll find in this characteristic Barcelona park. As you walk through the grounds of Park Guell, winding your way through the intricate, colorful paths, you will be amazed at the tiled beauty of the buildings, walls and small structures you come across. As you reach the peak of the park, you also gain unrestricted access to inspiring panoramic views of both the cityscape and nearby seaside, which on a clear day is even more beautiful than a work by Picasso himself.

Parc de la Ciutadella - To a real park in the more traditional sense, Parc de la Ciutadella is a hotspot for visitors of all ages and demographics at any time of the day. Many magnificent fountains and waterfalls feature throughout the park, there is more than enough room for a shaded picnic and there are a variety of sports to keep you busy: frisbee, roller blading and table tennis just to name a few.

Espit Chupitos - For any wild night in Barcelona, there is one bar which is sure to start the night off in the right direction. As you walk into Espit Chupitos, you will see a mass of avid party-goers lined up at a flaming bar, screaming and knocking back shots of every variety. At any one time, there are more shots on offer in this electric bar than people to drink them. With over 500 shots, including some savory, some sweet and some lit on fire before you drink them, this shots bar is anything but dull!

Font Magica - Yes this fountain is exactly what it sounds like: magical! Gushing with huge spouts of water, in an array of colors more dazzling than a rainbow, to the sounds of musical classics that are everyone's favorites, this fountain provides an experience that is in true Barcelona style. There are several shows throughout the night, all of which draw a phenomenal crowd to watch an exceptional performance. The Magic Fountain is the perfect finale to any adventurous day spent exploring this magnificent Spanish city.

Conclusion

Spain is a truly unique country full of amazing people to meet and experiences to be had. Unfortunately for most people, seeing the whole of Spain's wonderfully diverse country from top to bottom isn't a realistic option.

What I hope to have achieved with this book is to have provided you with a guide how to get the most out of Spain in whatever time you have to spend exploring it. I would encourage you to stay here for as long as possible and soak up everything the country has to offer; the cities, the people, the culture and every unforgettable experience. But if you can't, just make sure that you don't miss any of the cities I've mentioned and try to get to each of the sights I've listed.

If you can make this round trip of Spain and get to all of the sights mentioned, I can guarantee you that you will have had the experience of a lifetime, and will have captured a significant glimpse of Spain's powerful history, delicious cuisine, passionate people and unforgettable sights.

I have no doubt that you will return at some stage in the future, hungry to see more of the utterly inspiring country that is Spain.

Finally, if you enjoyed this book, please take the time to share your thoughts and post a review on Amazon. I would really appreciate it if you did.

Thank you and happy travels!

Printed in Great Britain
by Amazon